Pouring A Round Of Pensacola's Past

by
John D. Melvin, II

Pouring A Round Of Pensacola's Past

by
John D. Melvin, II

Pouring A Round Of Pensacola's Past
Copyright © 2017 by John D. Melvin, II

All rights reserved. No portion of this publication may be reproduced, stored in a retrieval system, or transmitted by any means—electronic, mechanical, photocopying, recording, or any other—except for brief quotations in printed reviews, without the prior written permission of the publisher.

All photographs, news clippings, and transcripts of news articles are the property of their respective owners and publications unless otherwise noted. Used with permission. Photographs courtesy of Pensacola Historical Society, University of West Florida Historic Trust.

Lead Editor: Hamishe Randall
Cover design: Amy Vega
Interior design: Lisa DeSpain
Cover Photographer: Chelsea Zachary

Indigo River Publishing
3 West Garden Street Ste. 352
Pensacola, FL 32502
www.indigoriverpublishing.com

Ordering Information:
Quantity sales: Special discounts are available on quantity purchases by corporations, associations, and others. For details, contact the publisher at the address above. Orders by U.S. trade bookstores and wholesalers: Please contact the publisher at the address above.

Printed in the United States of America

Library of Congress Control Number:
ISBN: 978-0-9972945-6-9
LOC: 2017933802
First Edition

With Indigo River Publishing, you can always expect great books, strong voices, and meaningful messages. Most importantly, you'll always find... words worth reading.

Dedication

This book is dedicated to Dr. Jay Clune, for his mentorship and unwavering support in all of my personal and academic endeavors, and for pushing me to never quit, even when it would have been very easy to do so. Doubtless, without Dr. Clune, I would not be where I am today. To him I owe my scholastic achievements, and I will forever be in his debt. Thank you, my friend.

Table of Contents

Pensacola: The Place to Be 1
Early German Influence 5
Kupfrian's Park 11
Early Saloons in Downtown Pensacola 21
Sam Clepper and Prohibition in Pensacola 31
The Spearman Brewing Company 43
The Brass Tacks: The Prominent Details in History 53
Pensacola Then and Now 59
Work Cited 73

Table of Figures

Figure 1 – Henry G.S. Baars (1844-1909) 6
Figure 2 – Conrad Kupfrian (1833-1892) 7
Figure 3 – Map of Kupfrian's Park (1914) 9
Figure 4 – Trolley to Kupfrian's Park (c. early 1900s) 10
Figure 5 – Christian Moerlein Brewing Company 12
Figure 6 – Festival at Kupfrian's Park (date unknown) 13
Figure 7 – Massive Oak Trees at Kupfrian's Park 14
Figure 8 – "Horseless Carriage" Race at
 Kupfrian's Park (date unknown) 15
Figure 9 – T.T. Wentworth Bicycle Ad 16
Figure 10 – Bartholomay Brewery 17
Figure 11 – Kupfrian's Park Picnic Area (date unknown) 18
Figure 12 – Automobile in Kupfrian's Park (c.1910s) 19
Figure 13 – Packed Grandstand at
 Kupfrian's Park (date unknown) 20
Figure 14 – Varieties Building
 (Photograph taken between 1870-1889) 25
Figure 15 – Capt. Jacob Kryger (1845-1908) 28
Figure 16 – Merchant's Hotel (1885) 29
Figure 17 – James Van Pelt (1864-1927) 33
Figure 18 – Anti-Saloon League Propaganda (c.1890s) 34

Figure 19 – Present Day Photograph of "The Barn" 38
Figure 20 – Recipe of John Edwards,
          Nephew of Herman Pfeiffer (April 1975) 41
Figure 21 – Guy M. Spearman (1896-1966) 44
Figure 22 – Spearman Brewing Company (date unknown) 46
Figure 23 – Spearman Straight Eight Beer Advertisement (1940) 47
Figure 24 – Spearman English Type Ale Advertisement (1947) 48
Figure 25 – Spearman Ace High Beer Bottle (1953) 51
Figure 26 – Spearman Cone-top and Traditional Beer Cans 51

Pensacola: The Place to Be

Pensacola is the nation's oldest settlement, and its economic and social history is thus rich and long lasting. Even after the American Civil War (1861-1865), when many major Southern cities were in utter shambles with the economic ravages the war reaped on the former Confederate States, Pensacola's pitch pine timber and lumber, brick making, and red snapper industries helped keep the city's economy afloat. Foremost among these industries, the lumber business boomed, lumber exports reached new all-time highs, and Pensacola shipping reached a scale never before fathomed. An environment existed in which social activities, in addition to commerce, burgeoned and left a notable imprint in the history of Pensacola. Rivaling major Northeastern cities in industrial and economic importance, the Port of Pensacola at old Palafox Wharf never rested. In fact, Pensacola was such an active port city that a legend arose: *one could walk across Pensacola Bay by jumping from one sailing vessel to another during the shipping boom in the late 19th century.* Although this legend is likely inaccurate, it gives insight into just how many ships inundated the bay on a daily basis.

Pouring A Round Of Pensacola's Past

By the 1880s, there was plenty of money in Pensacola, and there were also the right types of people to support a booming alcohol industry. The hope of prosperity—in a city full of as much promise as Pensacola—brought many ambitious, business-minded immigrants to Pensacola after the Civil War. One of these immigrants, Conrad Kupfrian (1833-1892), created a very popular park by 1878 in which alcohol became an important part of leisurely activity for countless Pensacolians. The Navy and the booming lumber and shipping industries also contributed to an environment in Downtown Pensacola that supported there being a saloon on seemingly every street corner. After all, both the Navy ships and the fishing smacks recruited their men from the saloons. Even during Prohibition, Pensacola still had its champion of the alcohol industry. While many cities' officials were giving in to the growing sentiment that alcohol was and should be outlawed at all costs, Pensacolians, in general—and Pensacola officials (the Escambia County Sheriff), in particular—did not make efforts to ban the sale of intoxicants until Prohibition became state law on January 1, 1919. Even after this crack down on the sale of alcohol, a bootlegger named Sam Clepper (1883-1957) became somewhat of a celebrity by defying the law and providing the well-to-do citizens of Pensacola with moonshine during the times of prohibition. Also, the Spearman Brewing Company, which was established in 1935 almost immediately after the repeal of prohibition, was initially a big economic success in Pensacola, and continues on as an important social facet in the world of can and bottle collecting. All four components of the alcohol industry—Kupfrian's Park with its German-style beer garden, the multitude of saloons that scattered Downtown Pensacola, prohibition in Pensacola and the bootlegger Sam Clepper's enterprise, and the Spearman Brewing Company—had major impacts on Pensacola's economy and society in the late 19th and early 20th centuries. Indeed, the money flowed in Pensacola, and so too did the booze.

Early German Influence

From the end of the Civil War to the turn of the 20th century, a large contingency of immigrants, many of whom were of German heritage, made Pensacola their new home. An example of such an early entrepreneur is Henry Gerhardt Sophus Baars (1844-1909). Henry Baars was from a German family, and in the 1850s, Germany was a warring state. But Henry's father bought him a replacement in the German army and sponsored young Henry in a shipping endeavor in Savannah, Georgia. His shipping efforts were interrupted by the American Civil War, in which he fought as a Confederate soldier. After the war, Baars was lured by the booming timber industry in Pensacola and opened an office for his shipping business, which was focused on pine lumber and naval stores. But it was not long before Baars turned his attention to real estate and made numerous land acquisitions; he acquired some 4,000 acres of land in the Cordova Park area throughout his life, launching the Baars real estate empire that still thrives today.

Another businessman and entrepreneur of German heritage who came to Pensacola during this time of economic development in hopes of making a name for himself was Conrad Kupfrian. Best known for the establishment of Kupfrian's Park and the Pensacola Street Car Company, Kupfrian made a significant contribution to Pensacola's social and economic history. Prior to the establishment of his famed park, Kupfrian's earliest enterprise in Pensacola was his saloon, the Globe House. Deed records show that in 1870, Conrad Kupfrian purchased lot 52 on Zaragoza Street from E. E. and Susan A. Simpson. Kupfrian most likely established his saloon on this tact of land.

Figure 1 – Henry G.S. Baars (1844-1909)

Figure 2 – Conrad Kupfrian (1833-1892)

Advertisements for the Globe House appeared in late 1883 and early 1884 in the *Pensacola Commercial News*. For example, one such advertisement indicates, "C. Kupfrian, Proprietor of Globe House, Zaragoza Street, Imported Wines and Liquors and cigars constantly on hand." Another related advertisement reveals, "C. Kupfrian, proprietor of the famous Globe House, has obtained the agency of C. Moerlein's celebrated bottled beer. The rush of custom to this place of business since the new acquisition is something wonderful and all who have partook of this beverage declare it to be the best in the market." Clearly, Kupfrian was proud of his German heritage, and he exploited his people's fondness for beer in his business endeavors;

it certainly did not hurt that this particular German beer happened to be one of the finest made at the time. Christian Moerlein Brewing Company was in fact one of the top twenty producers of beer in the United States by the time it became available at the Globe House. Indeed, Kupfrian's penchant for beer later followed him into his park, where he established a German-style beer garden, true to his family's heritage. Kupfrian made enough money with his saloon to help finance his next business endeavor, the Pensacola Street Car Company. This venture, in which he partnered with another fellow German businessman Henry Pfeiffer (1833-1887), later led right to the front gates of Kupfrian's most important undertaking: Kupfrian's Park—one end of the street car tracks ended at the front entrance of the park.

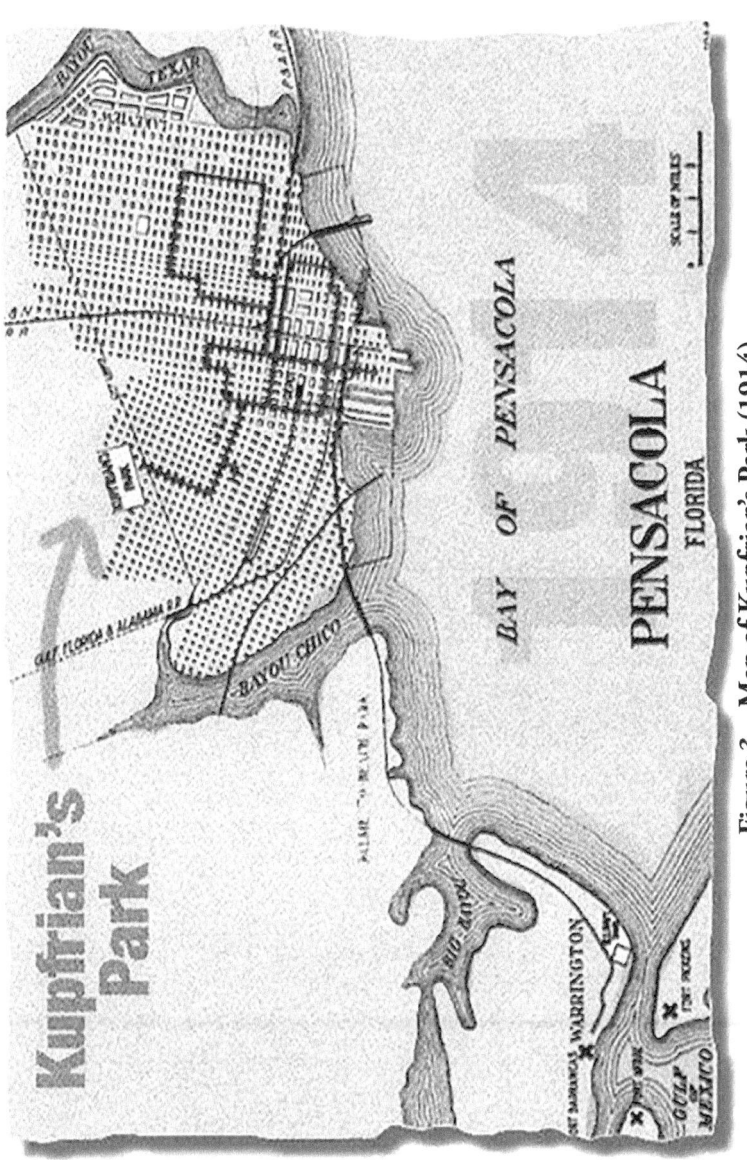

Figure 3 – Map of Kupfrian's Park (1914)

Figure 4 – Trolley to Kupfrian's Park (c. early 1900s)

Kupfrian's Park

Kupfrian's Park probably came into existence in 1878. County land records indicate that Conrad Kupfrian purchased approximately one hundred acres of land near present-day Baptist Hospital from George W. Reab in 1878 for $250. Later in the same year, Kupfrian purchased an additional tract of land, adjacent to the larger purchase, from Christian and B.E. Corner for the same price. Kupfrian soon built his park on this land, which apparently was already equipped with a complete racetrack around the central lake. A contemporary news story indicates that "the race track was completed in 1874," four years before Kupfrian purchased the land. The exact date Kupfrian established the park, however, is somewhat of a mystery. Nevertheless, one may surmise that Kupfrian had commenced with his new project by early 1884 (perhaps several years prior) as "the Pensacola City Directory of 1885 (the first published) listed Kupfrian as the proprietor of 'Kupfrian's Park,' as well as President of the Pensacola Street Car Co., and proprietor of a saloon on Zaragossa Street near Palafox Street." Also, an article in the *Pensacolian* of May 3, 1884 reveals what is perhaps the first recorded account of activities at the new park; the headline states, "Picnic at Kupfrian's splendid success." Doubtless, the German immigrant's traditional brew flowed out of his beer garden at such events.

Figure 5 – Christian Moerlein Brewing Company

During the time period following the Civil War, parks became a very popular form of entertainment in the Gulf Coast area. Many people visited Kupfrian's Park, Palmetto Beach, Casino Beach, Skinner's Park, Magnolia Bluff, and other nearby parks to pass time with their friends and families in the warm Florida weather; Pensacola was the place to be. Perhaps the oldest and most popular of all was Kupfrian's Park, a social gathering place with extensive recognition. Not only was Kupfrian's Park "the favorite pleasure resort of the tri-county tier of Baldwin, Escambia, and Santa Rosa," but also people from all over the South made it a point to visit Kupfrian's Park to fulfill their recreational needs. In fact, it is known that excursions from New Orleans frequently made the eastward trek in search for a release from life in the big city.

Figure 6 – Festival at Kupfrian's Park (date unknown)

Why was the park a "pleasure resort" of the tri-county area? Why did people come to Kupfrian's Park from as far as New Orleans during a time when such travel by horse and carriage or primitive automobile certainly was not a pleasure cruise in and of itself? Part of the answer to these questions lies in a town reporter's description of what Kupfrian's Park visitors saw upon arrival: "The grounds were well laid out, shaded by fine trees and within easy reach as the street cars are making regular trips to the park. Mr. Kupfrian spared neither expense nor trouble to make the park structure." Described as "a delightful place" in an 1895 issue of *Gulf Stream*, few could resist slipping away from the mundane, every-day toils of life into the worry-free environment of Kupfrian's Park.

Figure 7 – Massive Oak Trees at Kupfrian's Park

Furthermore, there were certainly many activities available to park visitors. With the large, half-mile dirt racetrack encircling an attention-grabbing central lake, races of all sorts were some of the most popular events at Kupfrian's Park. The park sponsored horse races throughout its earlier years. Shortly after its inception, the Pensacola Driving Association, a horse racing organization established in part by the fishing and maritime businessman Eugene E. Saunders (1845-1913) in April 1889, leased the Kupfrian's Park racetrack and held its first races on June 30, 1889. Over time, with the invention of the automobile, or "horseless carriage," and its rapid increase in popularity, horse racing became less and less frequent, and around 1910, "local sportsmen, including [Jack] Wright, Dr. S. R. Mallory Kennedy and F. M. Blount, began to race fast roadsters on the Kupfrian track."

Figure 8 – "Horseless Carriage" Race at Kupfrian's Park (date unknown)

In addition to horse and automobile racing, bicycle racing was also very popular at Kupfrian's Park. Theodore Thomas "T. T." Wentworth, Jr. (1898-1989) was a bicycle aficionado who promoted bicycle races at Kupfrian's Park from 1916 to 1920. The proprietor of a Pensacola bicycle shop, Wentworth organized a bicycle club (which may have been called the Pensacola Blades Bicycle Team) consisting of approximately one hundred members. During the racing season, every Sunday night Wentworth "conducted bicycle races for the club members." Track

Figure 9 – T.T. Wentworth Bicycle Ad

and field events were also sponsored at the park. In June 1895, the Pensacola Athletic Club held a track and field sporting event at Kupfrian's Park. The event program indicates "admission was $0.25…[and there] were such races as 100-yard dash, a one-mile run, and a tug of war for individuals, and a one-half mile bicycle race." Other recreational activities included baseball games, swimming in the lake, and boxing contests, in which only men participated. There are even accounts indicating dog and cockfights took place at Kupfrian's Park. Doubtless, park patrons could be entertained, enjoy various activities, and get plenty of exercise on any given day at Kupfrian's Park.

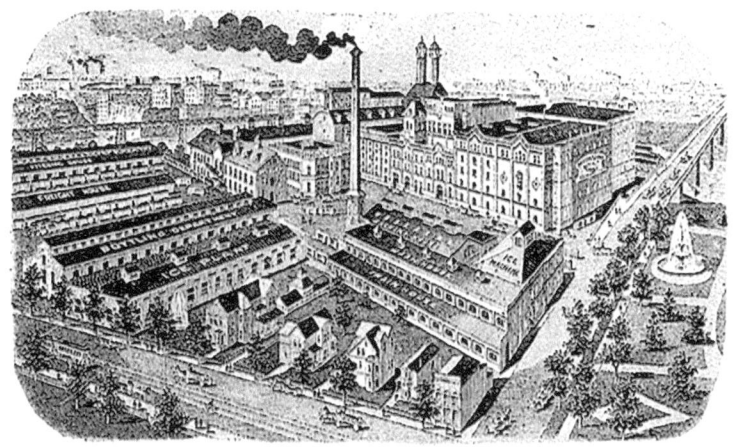

Bartholomay Brauerei

Figure 10 – Bartholomay Brewery

Aside from the recreational, competitive nature of park activities, Kupfrian's Park was also a beacon for social activities. With its many massive, old live oak trees and wooden tables and benches scattered about the park grounds, Kupfrian's Park was a haven for picnickers. Kupfrian used his past experience with his Globe House saloon and included a German-style beer hall in his park. Social gatherings, picnics, dances, and live music events were very common at Kupfrian's Park, and Kupfrian's German-style beer garden was put to good use on many occasions for such activities. An official programme for a race meet under the auspices of the West Florida Cycle and Good Roads Club, dated October 23, 1896, includes ads hoping to bolster business at the beer gardens during the sporting events. C. Moerlein beer is tagged as being the "Best Beer on the Market," while Indianapolis Beer is touted to be "The only Beer ever analyzed and found to be pure." And if park patrons

Figure 11 – Kupfrian's Park Picnic Area
(date unknown)

did not get their fill of fine German beer while enjoying the festivities, another portion of the programme states, "After the Races: Go to the GULF SALOON, Nos. 113 and 115 E. Zaragossa Street, and try a Glass or Bottle of that famous BARTHOLOMAY N.Y. BEER."

In addition to Kupfrian's beer, myriad other snacks and refreshments were available to park visitors. For five cents, patrons could purchase hot dogs or pork sandwiches. Furthermore, park visitors "could buy peanuts, popcorn, and wild grapes" to snack as they watched the races or listened to music at the bandstand, or took a break from dancing at the dance pavilion. A bandstand and dance pavilion added to the comforting atmosphere and provided for an even nicer place to have picnics. The park even "became the site of the annual Tri-County Fair, conducted by Baldwin County, Ala., and Escambia and Santa

Rosa Counties, Florida," and political rallies were not uncommon. Additionally, James R. McGovern, in his *Emergence of a City in the Modern South: Pensacola 1900-1945*, indicates that African-Americans "were given privileges to use...Kupfrian's Park on special nights of the week." Another source indicates there was, at one time, a dance pavilion used exclusively by African-Americans, but it burned down. During a time of racial discrimination, perhaps even black people found Kupfrian's Park a nice place to relax.

Figure 12 – Automobile in Kupfrian's Park (c.1910s)

Figure 13 – Packed Grandstand at Kupfrian's Park
(date unknown)

Early Saloons in Downtown Pensacola

Parks, such as Kupfrian's Park, were naturally a very popular early form of entertainment in the Pensacola area, and an excellent platform for a young German entrepreneur's ale. While the parks brought success and exposure, there were additional efforts in the 1870s to attract new residents to the Pensacola area, to bring in more money and help the city grow. For instance, one promotional tract proclaims, "As a place of residence, Pensacola is attractive by a healthy and genial climate. It has an abundance of excellent pure water, and the regularly changing land and sea breezes make it a pleasant abode at all seasons." While this description was not all truth, Pensacola undoubtedly had one great attribute: a top-notch harbor. The promotional tract did not adequately serve its purpose—to entice the elite; instead, as the lumber and shipping industries began to thrive, Pensacola "attracted roustabouts, prostitutes and sailors working off the frustrations caused by weeks at sea." Indeed, the two entities fed off one another. The saloons enjoyed the constant business, while the fishing smack captains and Navy recruiters consistently recruited new men out of the saloons. But, while the less desirable of society were occupying Downtown Pensacola, there was still a silver lining. As the shipping industry was booming and railroads were optimally utilized for timber transport, Pensacola quickly became a "first-class commercial city."

Furthermore, as Downtown Pensacola became more organized and populated, and as transportation methods—both public (street cars) and private (motorized carriages and automobiles)—advanced, citizens of Pensacola seemed to have taken their social interaction, and their beer-drinking, more from the outdoor setting of the park to the indoor setting of the saloon. In fact, by analyzing a small sampling of Pensacola city directories from 1893 to 1919, one can notice a sharp increase in alcohol-related business (particularly in the form of saloons) in the Pensacola area, followed by a decline and eventual end in official business with the passing of the statewide ban on the sale of alcohol in 1919. The directories do not actually list businesses specifically as "Saloons" until Maloney's *Pensacola City Directory (1898)*. The *Jones' Pensacola Directory (1893-1894)* only lists "Brewery Agents," "Wines and Liquors—Wholesale," and "Wines and Liquors—Retail." Listed under these categories, there are only three brewery agents, three wine and liquor wholesalers, and twenty-three wine and liquor retailers. The *Pensacola City Directory (1896)* lists four wine and liquor wholesalers—a slight increase from the previous issue—but lists twenty-one retailers, which is a slight decrease.

Maloney's Pensacola City Directory (1898) is a good indication that the alcohol industry in Pensacola had taken strong roots by the turn of the 20th century. In this issue, "Beer Agents" is a category, under which there are seven listings, and, for the first time, "Saloons" is a category, under which there are twenty-five listings. The *Wiggins' Pensacola City Directory* (1903) lists twenty-four saloons, a decrease of one from five years earlier, which indicates the saloon boom in Downtown Pensacola prior to prohibition did not occur immediately after the turn of the 20th century. However, just two years later, *R. L. Polk & Co.'s Pensacola Directory (1905)* shows that there were at least thirty saloons in operation, and even more interestingly, two years later, *R. L. Polk & Co.'s Pensacola Directory (1907)* lists thirty-nine saloons in operation. After 1907, the number of saloons seems to begin to drop; the 1908, 1909, 1911, and 1913 city directories all list the number of operating saloons in the low twenties. By 1916, there is no listing for "Saloons"; there are only listings for wines and liquors wholesale and retail. Of course, by 1919, with the passing of the statewide ban on the sale of alcoholic beverages, there is nothing alcohol-related listed in the Pensacola city directory.

Alcohol-related business was not only a way of making money during the late 19th and early 20th centuries; it was a way of life, with far-reaching social importance. The barroom of the time was nearly as common as the place of worship is today in Pensacola. In August 1974, Herman Pfeiffer recalled:

> Many years before the turn of this century and shortly thereafter there were saloons in every section of the city. One could be found on most every corner. They were more commonly called bars or barrooms. They were

easily identified by their swinging doors. There being a bar in most neighborhoods many take-out orders of draft beer were sold those days by the bucket or pitcher.

Pfeiffer also noted that there were many major breweries that supplied beer to the various saloons in Downtown Pensacola. For example, during this time when "bottle beer was packed in sawdust and shipped in barrels…[and] draft beer in kegs was shipped in railroad boxcars," Lion beer and Pabst Blue Ribbon (a brand still very popular today) were among the most commonly consumed. F. W. Brewing Co. of Gainesville, Indiana, a major contender in the brewing industry at the time, brewed Cooks beer, which was one of the most popular draft beers in Pensacola in the late 1800s. Also, Christian Moerlein Brewing Co. of Cincinnati, Ohio—which is known to have been immensely popular at Kupfrian's Park as well as many of the Downtown Pensacola saloons—was well liked at the time.

There were plenty of saloons in Downtown Pensacola during the late 19th and early 20th centuries, but what were they? Who were the people behind them? To analyze even a generous number of the numerous saloons that scattered the streets of Downtown Pensacola during this time of growth and change would require a book. However, there are several which are particularly worthy of discussing. Early in the lumber and shipping boom, Palafox Wharf naturally became a place of ruckus and nightlife; this is where the action was. Saloons of all sorts sprung up on both sides of Palafox Street, but two in particular were very unique.

Arthur and Maggie Quina, members of one of the prominent historic Pensacola families, were proprietors of the Royal Palace, located on the southeast corner of Magnolia and Palafox Streets. Interestingly, this business, which commenced operation around 1878—about the same time as Kupfrian's Park—was not an average saloon. Known as a "variety," the Royal Palace was a combination saloon, dancehall, and bordello. All of these activities were very common at the time in this part of the city, so why make patrons go elsewhere for their extracurricular pleasures? Charles Evans created a similar business one block north on the same street called the Bay View Variety Hall. Although Evans' establishment was consistently the venue for theatrical attractions and live bands, it was not

**Figure 14 – Varieties Building
(Photograph taken between 1870-1889)**

a safe place to be. In fact, both the Royal Palace and the Bay View Variety Hall "were the scenes of frequent spats and premeditated murders." The prior photograph shows one of these establishments; however, historical record cannot determine if it is the Royal Palace or the Bay View Variety Hall.

Another very important old-time saloon proprietor who had a significant influence on Pensacola's economy and society during the late 19th and early 20th centuries was Christian Ustrup Thiesen (1856-1934), for whom the Thiesen Building on Palafox Street is named. A native of Denmark, Thiesen made Pensacola his home in 1882 and began to purchase real estate in the Downtown area as investments the following year. Thiesen quickly became involved in the alcohol business; he operated "a saloon on the southwest corner of Baylen and Intendencia [Streets] as early as 1885, and continued as a barman through 1927." The *Pensacola City Directory (1896)* shows Thiesen as operating a second saloon located at 421 E. Garden Street. It is evident that Chris Thiesen took the business of operating his Baylen and Intendencia Street saloon very seriously. For example, "the rooms above the saloon where he lived became a home after his marriage to Gesina E. (Emilie) Lehnhuhl on June 12, 1884," and "The family [which, at the time, included seven children] lived over the saloon until Emilie died on January 21, 1900 from complications of childbirth." Thiesen took the saloon so seriously that he kept himself and his family virtually inseparable from the family business.

Chris Thiesen's alcohol-related enterprises in Downtown Pensacola are especially noteworthy. Thiesen contributed greatly to the economy by providing decades of local business, and he created two social gathering points where people from all levels of society congregated, whether they were rich or poor, white or black. One interesting detail regarding Chris Thiesen's saloons is that in all the years of his proprietorship, historical record reveals only one instance in which there is a court case involving disorderly conduct at one of his establishments (the saloon on the corner of Baylen and Intendencia Streets). On the evening of October 27, 1896, Officer Kelly overheard a drunken Peter Olsen arguing with another saloon patron, Bob King (a black man); "they were talking politics, discussing Silver and Gold, and McKinley and Bryan." The two men were separated and arrested and nobody was harmed. Thiesen was brought to court on the charge of "keeping a disorderly house" and was fined five dollars. So, even during a rough time in Pensacola's history, when saloons were quite dangerous and often even deadly places, Thiesen's establishment was a relatively safe social gathering place, where both white men and black men could go to enjoy a drink.

Captain Jacob Kryger (1845-1908) was yet another early saloon proprietor who helped to shape the alcohol industry in Pensacola during the late 19th and early 20th centuries. Captain Kryger was born in Germany and immigrated to the United States around 1872, "locating his family at Milton, and operating a freight schooner between New Orleans and Pensacola." After about four years, he ended his freight schooner business and "established a hotel at the corner of Government and Tarragonna Streets, which he operated for several years,

Figure 15 – Capt. Jacob Kryger (1845-1908)

when he purchased the Merchant's Hotel." Standing three stories tall and situated on the southwest corner of Government and Palafox Streets, the Merchant's Hotel was Kryger's largest alcohol-related enterprise, though it was not his only one. Kryger was also proprietor of the Bijou Saloon, which first appeared in the *Pensacola City Directory, 1896* as "LITTLE BJOU, 301 s. Palafox." Located in what was known as the Kryger Building, it is believed that the building was constructed shortly after the Civil War, and it is known to have been demolished in 1971. Herman Pfeiffer provided an enlightening description of the establishment, in the prime of the business, when Merchant's Hotel was going strong.

There were rooms on the second and third floors, Billiard Parlor, Barber Shop, Saloon, and Dining Room were on the bottom level. Actors and actresses began to lodge there after the opening of the Pensacola Opera House in 1883. Famous theatrical performers with names like John Drew, Richard Mansfield, Anna Pavola and Sarah Bernhardt were known to have registered there. It seems this hotel declined with the demolition of the Opera House.

This description shows exactly how an alcohol-related business venture—combined with lodging and entertainment interests—played an important part economically and socially in Pensacola.

Figure 16 – Merchant's Hotel (1885)

SAM CLEPPER AND PROHIBITION IN PENSACOLA

With the end of the First World War (1914-1918), Pensacola began to undergo many of the same social changes as the rest of the United States. As the so-called "Roaring Twenties" commenced, traditional social norms went more and more to the wayside. Although by this time, Pensacola, much like today, had become inundated with places of worship, many women embraced the new "flapper" persona, characterized by a more risqué manner of dress and an overall disregard for what had been previously considered as acceptable social behavior for women. After the great industrial boom of the late 19th century, Pensacola continued to develop. During the 1920s, Pensacola "experienced remarkable growth from rural in-migration," and by 1931, the city "had one church for every 404 residents." As James R. McGovern stated in his *The Emergence of a City in the Modern South: Pensacola 1900-1945*:

> Although ministers championed the enforcement of prohibition, Pensacolians generally did not respond

positively to their injunctions. Escambia County, largely as a result of its Pensacola vote, had been one of the four counties in the state of Florida to exercise local option and sell intoxicants until prohibition became state law, effective January 1, 1919. Even then, the law was challenged constitutionally by a Pensacola lawyer, Philip Beall. Indeed, the city's nonchalant compliance caused Governor Sidney J. Catts to appoint a special vigilante committee to bring about enforcement in the city and to remove the local sheriff, James Van Pelt.

It is clear that while prohibition had become the law of the land, Pensacola was not willing to change. Although the saloons that once scattered the streets of Downtown Pensacola—the same saloons that were at one time open for business almost all hours of the day—had officially been put out of business, Pensacola was not a city to easily give up its old ways, which had been so heavily influenced by the alcohol industry.

January 1920 marked the official beginning of the national prohibition of alcohol in the United States. Alcohol was immensely popular all over the country, especially in Pensacola. As a result, "speakeasies," or hidden booze halls, were established in many places in Pensacola. Angelo Maggio's at 414 W. Zarragossa Street was a much admired hangout at the time, and "the New Warrington Club operated by the illustrious R. G. 'Baby' Green, or George Wilson's Pioneer Roadhouse on Gulf Beach Highway," were also popular speakeasies during prohibition in Pensacola. Also, it is known that some "soda shops" and filling stations sold moonshine, and one "local prohibition

Figure 17 – James Van Pelt (1864-1927)

agent himself was arrested for selling liquor." While alcohol was illegal, some of the larger breweries did make efforts to create a substitute known as "near beer," with trace amounts of alcohol, to satisfy the appetite of the populace. This concept flopped, however, as people began making their own booze with larger amounts of alcohol. Prohibition created an illegal atmosphere in which the common people were inclined to concoct liquor or beer in their own back yards in order to whet their appetites and turn profit as the demand for quality alcohol was on the rise.

The Anti-Saloon League, a temperance group launched in 1893, became a popular organization in Pensacola long before prohibition officially took effect. A foundation of reform groups since the Second Great Awakening, temperance "became an even greater issue during the Progressive Era as the influx of immigrants into the United States made alcohol consumption a battleground between 'drys,' who were often native born, and 'wets,' who were often immigrants; the typical 'wet' was a German brewer or saloon owner." Indeed, Conrad Kupfrian, Chris Thiesen, and Jacob Kryger were only a few of many men who fell into this category. In an effort to persuade as many Pensacolians as possible to abide by the tenets of anti-alcoholism, the Anti-Saloon League utilized the myriad churches as their forum. Nevertheless, with the efforts of the Anti-Saloon League, and "after the passage of the national prohibition amendment, Pensacola still had a reputation for being a place where booze was available."

Figure 18 – Anti-Saloon League Propaganda (c.1890s)

Booze of all sorts was available, certainly not just beer. Pensacola's bustling port was not limited to the legitimate business ventures of pitch pine timber and lumber and red snapper. Smuggling of illegal intoxicants from Cuba into Pensacola's port was common, as became evident by the "occasional cache of rum bottles which would pop to the surface of the water and be confiscated." Moonshine, or "shinny" as it was commonly called at the time, also became popular in Pensacola, primarily because of the large European population. The dense woods of Escambia County became a haven for moonshiners to produce their prized shine. The Ard family became one of the most well known families in Pensacola during this time for their exploits in the alcohol business. The Ards were from the west side of Pensacola and utilized the western farmlands to grow abundant supplies of corn, but they were not concerned about making corn meal or grits. The Ards took their entire crop and made corn whiskey, and during prohibition, they were known for making some of the finest whiskey in Pensacola. Though the Ards became famous during this time period, perhaps nobody became as well known as the bootlegger Sam Clepper.

Before discussing Sam Clepper, one may get an idea for how busy the illicit alcohol business was in Pensacola during prohibition by analyzing some newspaper articles from the time period. For example, one 1926 *The Pensacola Journal* article, titled "Raiders Continue to Seize Liquor Stills in the County," identifies three men—J. F. Godwin, Nathan Balcolman, and T. J. Williams—as being arrested on charges of moonshining. The article indicates "ten gallons of alleged moonshine whiskey and a ten barrel outfit was confiscated in a raid...according to an announcement by R. S. Stearns, prohibition officer." Furthermore, another article from the next day's paper, titled "Prohibition Men Take Big Still," reveals a little more about the same story, indicating that the fully operational outfit Godwin, Balcolman, and Williams were running contained "ten barrels of mash and a two-hundred gallon still." This certainly was not a small operation. Yet another article from the same paper later that year reveals that incidents involving illicit alcohol were not limited to the land. "Liquor Runners May Have Taken Agents in Tow" describes the efforts of law enforcement agencies in apprehending a three-masted schooner, which was suspected to have been a rumrunner with two prohibition agents on board held as captives.

One oral history account really gives a glimpse into the commonplace nature of alcohol production amongst ordinary people in Pensacola during prohibition. While doing research on the experiences of Pensacola women during the Great Depression of the 1930s, Elizabeth Vickers of the University of West Florida interviewed Mrs. Violet Aldridge who, at the time of the interview, was eighty-one years old. Mrs. Aldridge recounted that one winter her brother was caught by a policeman while getting coal from a coal car at the railroad tracks, which he was not supposed to be doing. Luckily, however, he was not arrested. "Daddy knew just about all the policemen down there... Momma made the home brew and half the policemen come there and drink it." Mrs. Aldridge's daughter participated in the oral history and stated that her parents sold the beer to the policemen, which explains why her brother was not arrested when he had broken the law.

These are just some examples of instances in which the common man created his own alcoholic beverage, whether beer or moonshine, in his own backyard, for his own consumption or for sale to others who were likely in a similar social class. It was the money of the more prominent citizens of Pensacola, however, that really helped drive the illegal alcohol business during prohibition, and there was one man in particular to whom they turned for product: Sam Clepper. As McGovern states, "For the well-to-do, who desired service, Sam Clepper was courteous enough to deliver a jug in a brown box; those willing to cash and carry could obtain a five-gallon keg for ten dollars by driving in the direction of Clepper's place near Perdido Bay."

Although historical record does not reveal much about Sam Clepper the man, many accounts are available, both written and oral, describing some of his clients. For instance, in a document titled "The Barn," written by J. Brent Watson, the author describes The Barn as a building located at 105 W. Jackson Street, which was purchased by his grandfather in 1909. From 1928 to 1933, during prohibition, the building was rented as an officer's club, and officers, flight instructors, and flight students attended many functions at The Barn "for parties, dancing, drinks, and so forth." Watson notes that the Navy purchased their own moonshine for these functions from the well-known bootlegger Sam Clepper, and through all the festivities, the federal officers never bothered anybody. Capt. Roscoe Lee Newman, USN, Ret. was also known to attend the get-togethers at The Barn. In his document, Watson quotes Capt. Newman: "There were some great, real booming get-togethers at The Barn. Mrs. Will Davis and her two daughters, Jessie and Flossie used to invite a few of us young fellows for a ritual with dinner and homemade beer. The ritual was 'make a batch, bottle a batch, and drink a batch'." Even a Captain in the United States Navy enjoyed alcohol-friendly parties during prohibition and partook of Sam Clepper's celebrated whiskey and some old fashioned home brewed beer.

Figure 19 – Present Day Photograph of "The Barn"

Another piece of information regarding Sam Clepper—or at least his famous whiskey—which has been left in historical record is found in a February 19, 1996 letter written to the Pensacola Historical Society from William S. Rosasco, III.

> As a very young boy I can remember when one afternoon Dad (William S. Rosasco, Jr.) allowed me to go visit with

him. Of course I went and of course I didn't know where the ultimate destination would be. But I do remember we pulled up and dad stopped the car and opened his trunk and there was a large keg that was placed in the trunk and we came home. Then the keg was carried into the house where he had built a ladder that you could get to the ceiling and then you would simply push the 3x3 door to the side and that's where Dad would store the keg of Sam Clepper's whiskey. It would stay there usually until the Christmas celebration.

Rosasco continues in his letter that his family did not only enjoy the famous Sam Clepper whiskey during holiday celebrations. During the days of Sam Clepper, trade between Genoa, Italy and Pensacola was strong; shipping vessels constantly entered the port at Pensacola bringing in various goods from Italy and returning with heart pine, which had been a booming business in Pensacola since the 1880s. Rosasco notes that as the Italians were in town picking up products to bring back to their home country, his father put Sam Clepper's famous whiskey in quart bottles, decorated the bottles with Rosasco Brothers labels, and gifted them "to those who were supplying the heart pine that was purchased by the Rosasco Brothers and sold in Genoa, Italy where the firm's office was located." This was apparently common practice amongst other major companies in Pensacola at the time.

One final point of information about Sam Clepper is somewhat anecdotal in nature, but it is important nevertheless. Upon interviewing Lee Hual of Pensacola, she revealed an interesting facet of Sam Clepper's life. Mrs. Hual stated that Clepper was a bootlegger and moonshiner during prohibition in Pensacola and was known for making some of the finest "shinny" in town, which is a well-known fact. She also stated that many of the homes in the North Hill area had basements, and many barrels of moonshine were delivered to her uncle Richard Hill Turner at 300 W. Gonzalez Street and his brother across the street at 301 W. Gonzalez Street, and it was their children's job to go down to the basement every so often to turn the kegs to keep the moonshine fresh. But to what extent was Clepper raised to somewhat of a "celebrity status" because of the importance of his business and the quality of his product during the time of prohibition? According to Mrs. Hual, Clepper was thought of very highly by the well to do in society for his quality moonshine, but the judge, though he himself was a paying customer, had to put Clepper in jail for his illegal activities.

While in jail, people made every effort to make sure Sam Clepper was comfortable and taken care of. For instance, Marion Albert Quina ("Papa Quina"), Lee Hual's maternal grandfather, who owned a stevedoring company in Pensacola and lived on Lee Square, always insisted that Lee's mother—who was about thirteen years old at the time—deliver Sam Clepper food in his jail cell when the Quina family enjoyed Sunday dinner. Mrs. Hual's grandmother, seeing Sam Clepper as nothing more than a common criminal, did not like the thought of her daughter bringing him Sunday dinner and denied her the right to do so. Mrs. Hual confirmed that her mother probably never actually delivered Sam Clepper dinner in jail, per her mother's request.

However, the dinner was almost certainly prepared and was very likely delivered to Clepper by her grandfather, "Papa Quina." Records indicate that a "Samuel Clepper," who died in 1957, is interred in Union Hill Cemetery in Myrtle Grove, and one can only believe that this is *the* Sam Clepper, the legendary Pensacola bootlegger.

> To begin a batch was simple. You needed to purchase a crock, capper and dozens of beer bottles, dark bottles preferable. To each can of malt and hops you added one yeast cake and five pounds of sugar. This mixture was stirred in luke warm water to dissolve. The contents then were poured into the five gallon crock filled with water. It was then set in a dark warm room to ferment. To add rice or potatoes was optional. It was thought to add either gave the brew more kick. It took 7 to 12 days to ferment. A hydrometer was used for testing. If red mark was reached brew was ready for bottling. You added 1/4 teaspoon sugar to each bottle when bottling. Each day foam was strained off top of batch while fermenting. You never stirred it while it was working. Five gallon batch made fifty to fifty five bottles of beer. The most popular brands of malt was Red Top, Budweiser and Heidelberg.
>
> While waiting for brew to ferment bottles were washed and sterilized. Pebbles shook well in bottles when washing removed caked yeast sediments. When brew was ready for bottling you elevated the crock higher than the bottles; placing a small rubber tube or hose in crock you then sucked on the hose to start the flow of beer to fill bottles. A clamp on the hose allowed you to stop flow between the filling of each bottle.
>
> The bottle capper reminded one of a large nut cracker. It was a simple device. It stood high enough for a tall beer bottle to be set under its tallest part. The cap would be placed on the mouth of the bottle. The lever on the capper was pressed. That lowered the head of the capper to the bottle. It fastened the cap tightly.

Figure 20 – Recipe of John Edwards, Nephew of Herman Pfeiffer (April 1975)

The Spearman Brewing Company

Throughout the period of prohibition, the alcohol business in Pensacola was in full swing, thanks to the efforts of such people as Sam Clepper and the Ard family, along with the financial backing of primarily the well-to-do citizens of Pensacola. Although alcohol was still accessible during prohibition, it was a relief for all beer drinkers when the ban was lifted in 1933, and people could once again visit the nearest pub or convenience store, rather than sneak into a speakeasy to enjoy an intoxicating beverage. But more than just legal alcohol came to the citizens of Pensacola upon the repeal of prohibition. In 1929, just a few years before the ban was lifted, the Georgia-born businessman Guy M. Spearman (1896-1966) came to Pensacola with hopes of making a name for himself in the ice business. Upon arriving to Pensacola, Spearman purchased the Crystal Ice Company, but "after due consideration and several trips to Monterrey, Mexico, to visit the Carta Blanca Brewery there, [Spearman] decided to go into the brewing business." By the end of 1934, the plans for the new Spearman Brewing

Company—which was constructed at 1600 S. Barrancas Avenue—were finalized, and "beer production began May 10, 1935, approximately two years after the repeal of prohibition." The citizens of Pensacola now had a hometown brew they could legally enjoy without fear of repercussion. Spearman, in a sense, became the new Sam Clepper, the go-to guy for all of one's local alcohol needs in Pensacola. Only at this time, the beverage did not have to be personally delivered by Guy Spearman in a brown box or secretively consumed in private clubs. It was indeed the beginning of a new era in the alcohol industry in Pensacola, and the Spearman Brewing Company was there to help pave the way.

Figure 21 – Guy M. Spearman (1896-1966)

John D. Melvin, II

From the earliest part of his life, Guy Spearman prepared himself academically for success in the business realm. He graduated from Cordova High School in Birmingham, Alabama, and later received his mechanical engineering degree from the Alabama Polytechnic Institute at Auburn in 1914. His education and natural leadership abilities led him into the proprietorship of a company that had a major influence on Pensacola for many years to come. The initial impact the company had on Pensacola was mostly economic. In its first year of operation, the Spearman Brewing Company employed approximately fifty employees. Over the next two years of operation, "production nearly doubled in volume and the workforce grew from 50 to 80 men. The plant was expanded three times and between November, 1935, and October, 1936, over 47 million bottles of beer were produced." Though it was considered a relatively small operation, producing around 500,000 barrels of ale per year, the Spearman Brewing Company "was one of a network of small beer makers that produced 46 percent of the nation's beer at one time." At its peak production during the Second World War, the Spearman Brewing Company employed over 150 employees to produce the immensely popular beer and ale. Thus it is clear that Spearman provided the citizens of Pensacola with much more than alcoholic beverages after prohibition; he provided them hometown pride and local jobs.

Indeed, Pensacola was at it again. The small, post-bellum Southern city had made a name for itself in the pitch pine timber and lumber, brick making, and red snapper industries during the latter part of the 19th century, and Spearman's brewing

Figure 22 – Spearman Brewing Company (date unknown)

company was on the verge of making Pensacola famous. Initially, the Spearman Brewing Company only produced keg beer, but the demand for smaller containers increased dramatically. In response, Spearman made the proper adjustments to meet the changing demands, and within two years he added a bottling plant to his company. But Guy Spearman did not stop at the addition of a bottling facility; he continued to pour resources into his business in order to make it the best around. In its formative years, "Spearman Brewing Company was one of the most modern small breweries in the South. It was considered to be one of the leading small breweries in the country. The plant was said to have covered two city blocks and contained the only floorless, four-story aging cellar in the south." Needless to say, the Spearman Brewing Company had a major impact on Pensacola's economy and society during its time.

What is perhaps most interesting about Spearman's brewing company is the amount of creativity he put into his marketing and presentation. Guy Spearman was proud of the fact that the Spearman Brewing Company was located in historic Pensacola, and he decided to let Pensacola's history help his business become as successful as possible. For example, in the company's early years, "the Spearman labels carried the five flags insignia representing the flags of the government under which Florida has been administered. This insignia was later adopted by the City of Pensacola, while Spearman soon after adopted the profile of Ponce de Leon," the famed explorer who once sought the "Fountain of Youth."

Figure 23 – Spearman Straight Eight Beer Advertisement (1940)

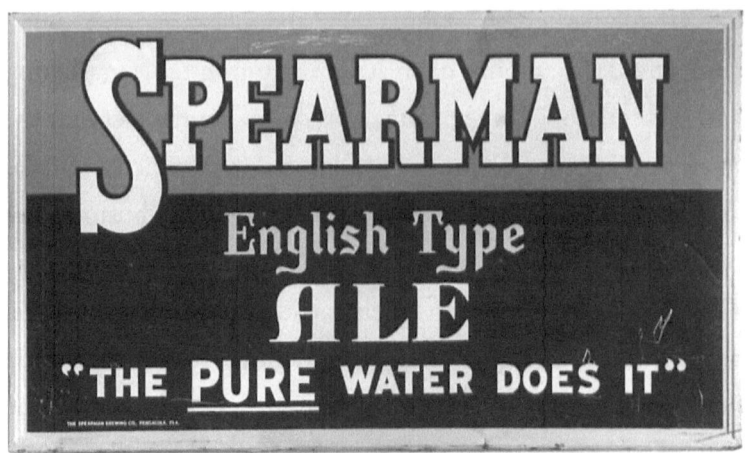

Figure 24 – Spearman English Type Ale Advertisement (1947)

The first beer the Spearman Brewing Company produced in bottles was dated May 10, 1935—it was called Spearman Straight 8 Beer, and by 1949, more label changes occurred along with additional products called Ace High Ale and English Type Ale, which both came in bottles and cans. "The Water Does It" is a reference to the pure water—which was drawn from wells on Spearman facility property—the Spearman Brewing Company used in producing its beer and ale, and in 1949, the company announced that it spent $100,000 per year on advertising Spearman products and the pure Pensacola well water from which the beer and ale was made. The advertising campaign was widespread, reaching as far East as St. Augustine, as far North as Birmingham, Alabama, and as far West as Biloxi, Mississippi.

The Spearman Brewing Company continued on in Pensacola for over twenty years under the auspices of its founder, Guy

Spearman. Over these years, the company played a part in helping to revitalize the city, socially and economically. Hundreds of thousands of barrels of high quality beer and ale rolled off the plant floors each year and was enjoyed by Pensacolians and people all over the Southeast region, and many people in Pensacola gained a new sense of pride because of the success of the hometown operation. Additionally, the brewing operation created hundreds of local jobs over the company's period of operation, which doubtless was a helpful boost to Pensacola's economy.

Operations ran relatively smoothly for Guy Spearman until the 1950s, when sales began to decrease, partially because of competition from big-name beer brands. The beer man decided to get out of the brewing industry while business was lagging in order to focus his attention on his ice company, which he had been running concurrently the entire time. Guy M. Spearman, Jr., the brewery proprietor's son, later recalled, "The expenses were great. Sales were small." He added that his father "just decided to get out while he didn't owe anybody anything." Spearman pulled out completely when he sold his company to the Hertzberg Foundation in 1955. The Hertzberg Foundation "continued to produce Spearman products, but sometimes used other company names and other locations." For instance, the new owners continued to produce Spearman Beer, Spearman Ale, and Viking Ale in Pensacola as well as other locations throughout the country. Additionally, "Spearman product names have appeared on cans bearing the names of Sewanee Brewing Company of Pensacola, Century Brewing of Norfolk, Virginia and elsewhere."

Pouring A Round Of Pensacola's Past

The discussion hitherto has focused mostly upon the economic importance of the Spearman Brewing Company. However, one of the longest lasting—and perhaps one of the most important—contributions the company made to society over the past half century lies in a simple hobby: can and bottle collecting. Lengthy and in-depth publications in the mid-1980s, such as *The Beer Can Collectors News Report* and *The American Can Collector*, show the magnitude of the hobby nationwide. Special features in which the Spearman Brewing Company is singled out, with front page photographs and pictures of beer cans throughout most of the pages of the publication indicate the importance of the company within the industry. Spearman's cans have become quite valuable over the years. For instance, in 1986, a Spearman English Type Ale cone-top can was valued in *The American Can Collector* at $180 and up, and a Spearman Beer cone-top can featuring the Ponce de Leon insignia on the top-front of the can was appraised at over $200. The photograph below presents a wide array of Spearman beer and ale cans throughout the years. The aforementioned "cone-top" style of can is distinctly evident, compared to the more traditional cylindrical cans.

Figure 25 – Spearman Ace High Beer Bottle (1953)

Figure 26 – Spearman Cone-top and Traditional Beer Cans

The Brass Tacks: The Prominent Details in History

Throughout Pensacola's long and rich history, the booming alcohol industry that ensued between the inception of Kupfrian's Park (1878) and the founding of the Spearman Brewing Company (1935) has not been excessively analyzed, though it is a very important part of the city's history. Pensacola's pitch pine timber and lumber, brick making, and red snapper industries helped the city's economy develop after the Civil War, while many other post-bellum Southern cities struggled. Pensacola's timber shipping industry soared during the 1880s and 1890s, and even into the new century, and these times of economic prosperity ushered in an environment that supported a flourishing alcohol industry. Thus it is clear that the history of Pensacola transcends in importance the mere fact that it is the oldest attempted settlement in the United States. The exciting times in the late 19th and early 20th centuries are also very interesting and equally important, for the alcohol industry in Pensacola—particularly Kupfrian's Park with his famous German-style beer garden, the myriad saloons that inundated Downtown Pensacola, the prohibition-related establishments and activities (including the efforts of the bootlegger Sam Clepper), and the Spearman Brewing Company—had a major impact on Pensacola's economy and society during this pivotal time in Pensacola's history.

Parks became a very popular form of entertainment in the Gulf Coast area following the Civil War. People often visited Palmetto Beach, Casino Beach, Skinner's Park, Magnolia Bluff, and other popular parks to pass the time in the warm Florida weather, but perhaps the most popular recreational area of all was Kupfrian's Park. Conrad Kupfrian created his park around 1878, shortly after starting his Globe House saloon business, as a beacon for social and recreational activity. The beautiful park, scattered with large live oak trees and picnic tables, was home to many different sporting events—such as bicycle racing, baseball, boxing, and track and field events—and it was the place for countless social activities, including picnics, dances, and live music events. Not only did Pensacolians enjoy the splendors of Kupfrian's Park, but also people from all over the South (even as far West as New Orleans) traveled to Pensacola to visit the pleasure resort. It was at the recreational and social events that Kupfrian bolstered support for his German-style beer garden, and it became immensely popular. The alcohol industry was indeed alive and well at Kupfrian's Park, and it is clear that Kupfrian's beer gardens greatly influenced both social activity and the economy in Pensacola for many years during the latter part of the 19th century.

John D. Melvin, II

The timber shipping industry in Pensacola during the 1880s was booming, and money was beginning to pour into the city. Many business-minded entrepreneurs, much like Conrad Kupfrian, made their way to Pensacola in hopes of making their dreams of prosperity come true. Countless immigrants who came to Pensacola during the time were of European (particularly German) heritage, and beer and liquor were quite literally in their blood. Christian Ustrup Thiesen and Capt. Jacob Kryger were two men of German descent who were determined to become successful businessmen in Pensacola as saloon proprietors, and they became two of the most successful. Thus, the influx of immigrants and entrepreneurs of all sorts into Pensacola during this time of economic prosperity created an environment that could easily support a large number of saloons in Downtown Pensacola.

Additionally, the thriving industry at the Port of Pensacola at old Palafox Wharf and the presence of the Navy helped to ensure the multitude of saloons in the area could thrive. The saloons enjoyed the constant business from fishing smack crews and Navy sailors, while the fishing smack captains and Navy recruiters constantly recruited new men out of the saloons. Economically, it is obvious how the alcohol industry had an impact on Pensacola in regard to the Downtown saloons, but one can more easily understand the social impact when one considers such establishments as Arthur and Maggie Quina's Royal Palace "variety" and Charles Evans' Bay View Variety Hall—both combination saloon, dance hall, and bordello—or even Christian Thiesen's saloon on Baylen and Intendencia Streets, which is known to have been an establishment where people of all races congregated for drinks and social activity on a daily basis, with only one recorded incident that led to an arrest.

Prohibition certainly hurt the Downtown saloon business in Pensacola, but it did not adversely affect the alcohol industry as a whole. It essentially altered the way the industry operated, just like in any other city around the country, except Pensacola was perhaps less willing than many other cities to give in to the tenets of anti-alcoholism, to abide by the laws of prohibition. After all, the alcohol industry had been such an important part of life for the city for the past half century. Speakeasies sprung up all over the city. Angelo Maggio's, the New Warrington Club, and George Wilson's Pioneer Roadhouse were only a few of the popular speakeasies in Pensacola during prohibition. For those who did not want to rely on private, hidden clubs for their booze, home brewing and moonshining became very common. Also, Sam Clepper and the Ard family were great sources for high quality liquor during prohibition for those who wanted to enjoy their intoxicants in the comfort of their homes but could not, or did not want to, manufacture their own moonshine. The time period of prohibition, which was mostly the "roaring twenties," was an incredible time, indeed. Social activity flourished during this time, as people drank their illegal beverages in private clubs, or purchased large quantities of Sam Clepper's famous moonshine for parties and family get-togethers, and the money flowed just as much as the booze.

Finally, the Spearman Brewing Company had an immense impact on Pensacola, both economically and socially.

John D. Melvin, II

Established in 1935, shortly after the repeal of prohibition, the Spearman Brewing Company's initial influence was largely economic. Starting with approximately 50 employees, the workforce increased to about 80 people over the next two years; thus, the new brewing operation not only provided the citizens of Pensacola with a hometown brew which they could enjoy and be proud of, but it also provided the city many jobs and a lot of revenue. By the Second World War, some 150 employees worked at the Spearman Brewing Company, as the factory produced approximately a half million barrels of beer and ale per year. Guy Spearman continued to develop and operate the company relatively smoothly until the 1950s when, amidst a period of lagging sales, he decided to sell the business in 1955. The Spearman Brewing Company continues to play an important role socially, however, as many of Spearman's bottles and cans have become quite collectable over the years. Also, although Pensacola is widely known as the "City of Five Flags," it is apparent that Guy Spearman adopted the "five flags" insignia for his initial beer label before Pensacola utilized the famed motif. Indeed, the Spearman Brewing Company will long be remembered as the significant little brewing operation that almost made Pensacola famous.

Pensacola Then and Now

Clearly, Pensacola's history is rich and long-lasting, and the alcohol industry has had a significant contribution on economic and social change for generations. From the early German immigrants, such as Conrad Kupfrian and Henry Gerhardt Sophus Baars, to moonshine distributors and beer brewers, like Sam Clepper and Guy Spearman, alcohol has played a significant role in shaping the culture of Pensacola. As far back as the late 19th century, people visited Pensacola from all over the Southeast to experience a city steeped in what could almost be considered magical qualities. Initially, the pleasant Gulf air and beautiful, massive live oak trees presented Pensacola in a picturesque fashion. Later, the "pure water" is what brought Pensacola notoriety as renowned local beer brewing burgeoned. Regardless of what brought people to Pensacola, there was one unremitting theme: Pensacolians had a penchant for alcohol.

But what has become of the alcohol industry in Pensacola in the early 21st century? Well, in short, alcohol continues to play a significant role in Pensacola's social and economic climates.

Pouring A Round Of Pensacola's Past

Pensacola boasts some of the country's most beautiful white-sand beaches. Pensacola's rich history also attracts tourists from near and far. From the National Museum of Naval Aviation to the historical remains of the Civil War relic Fort Pickens, history enthusiasts are welcomed with an array of entertaining and educational sites and activities.

Today, instead of going to parks, like Kupfrian's Park, or whiling the hours away in saloons, like the Globe House or Thiesen's saloon, folks are inclined to visit one of Pensacola's many fine-dining restaurants. The importance of alcohol in today's society is still quite evident. In fact, several alcoholic beverages—distinct to Pensacola—have gained quite a bit of notoriety. For instance, at McGuire's Irish Pub, visitors can sip on an *Irish Wake*. This highly intoxicating drink, consisting of a generous portion of rum and liqueur, packs such a punch that McGuire's has officially instituted a rule that limits three Irish Wakes per person. At Flounders Chowder House, located on Pensacola Beach, one can enjoy another Pensacola original:

the *Diesel Fuel*. Served in a large Mason jar, similar to the Irish Wake, the Diesel Fuel is equally as potent. It is essentially a large Long Island Iced Tea without tequila. If one is in the mood for something as sweet as it is alcoholic, The Sandshaker Lounge, which is also located on Pensacola Beach, has just the thing: the *Bushwacker*. Known as "The Home of the Original Bushwacker," the Sandshaker Lounge has been churning out its signature drink for over 30 years. Invented in Pensacola in 1975, the Bushwacker is a sweet, milkshake-like delicacy comprised of coffee liqueur and rum.

When the sun goes down in Pensacola, the nightlife comes alive. In recent times, there has been a revitalization of Downtown Pensacola. Once a haven for action-seekers and alcohol-drinkers—when there was a saloon on nearly every street corner—Downtown Pensacola experienced an economic and social decline that lasted nearly a century. However, once again, Pensacola's thriving Downtown community is bringing recognition back to the city as "the place to be" for food, fun, and beverage. With this reemergence has come an array of social activities and establishments that are once again bringing people from all over the Southeast. For instance, Palafox Street, which once boasted varieties, saloons, and speakeasies, is now characterized by a distinctly attractive selection of fine-dining establishments, modern bars, upscale clothiers, music halls, theaters, and art galleries.

Indeed, Pensacola has once again become a prime spot for alcohol-related events. In bygone days of Pensacola's postbellum glory, beer enthusiasts may have visited Kupfrian's Park to sample some of Christian Moerlein's finest ale, or to imbibe on classic Pabst Blue Ribbon. A similar scenario exists today, and generations later, Pabst Blue Ribbon continues to pour from the taps. But, rather than visiting German-style beer gardens dispersed amongst park grounds, Pensacola beer drinkers can visit the many local breweries and tap rooms, and may now participate in any of the myriad alcohol-related festivals. Pensacola is host to the annual Emerald Coast Beer Festival, which takes place at historic Seville Quarter. Ticket-holders can get their fill of dozens of beers, from nationally renowned brewing companies and local home brewers alike. Of course, the presence of the alcohol industry in Pensacola transcends merely beer. Pensacola also hosts annual wine, martini, and Bushwacker festivals.

So what does the future hold for the alcohol industry in Pensacola? Of course, only time will tell. Throughout the United States, let alone Pensacola, state and local ordinances are chipping away at many of our long-enjoyed "vices" in piecemeal fashion. Although the bulk of governmental efforts to stifle certain freedoms that may be considered "distasteful" are focused more upon the tobacco industry, anti-alcohol litigation at the local level does not go unnoticed. From the so-called "blue laws," which ban the sale of alcohol on Sundays, to the open container restrictions, which forbid the possession of open alcoholic beverages on Pensacola Beach central commercial areas (alcohol is limited to the sandy areas on the beach waters) limitations upon Pensacola's thriving alcohol industry are apparent. But, like the old sayings about history repeating itself go, if the alcohol industry in Pensacola thrived even during prohibition, there is little doubt that Pensacolians and tourists will continue to *pour another round* in this historical city for a long time to come.

Continuing Tradition: The Beer Brewers of Modern Pensacola

In light of Pensacola's potable past, I would be remiss if more of this book was not dedicated to the present-day beer brewers of Pensacola…

Gulf Coast Brewery

This beautiful brewpub is a haven for folks seeking a comfortable and relaxing—yet equally refined and upscale—atmosphere to enjoy their craft brews. Gulf Coast Brewery is a microbrewery with a penchant for exceeding expectations. Founded by Elliott Eckland in 2015, this picturesque pub epitomizes the notion of community togetherness built upon a foundation of premium, fresh-brewed beer. Gulf Coast Brewery is characterized by its diversification. A walk-in humidor houses a selection

of premium, hand-made cigars. Patrons can pair their fresh brewed beer with a premium cigar and relax amid friends in the luxurious smoking lounge. Cigar lockers are also available for those cigar connoisseurs who prefer to store their collection of smokes on site, always conveniently available in the smoking lounge. There is also an elegant wine lounge to compliment the extensive wine list. Here, customers can enjoy their favorite wine by the glass or bottle. The brewery even offers an outdoor patio area for folks who prefer the great outdoors.

The pride and joy of Gulf Coast Brewery is its fresh-brewed, premium beer. The brewing operation is truly remarkable. Owner and master brewer Elliott Eckland has a deep love for German-style beer, but his selection transcends the usual Bock, Dunkel, Hefeweizen, and Pilsner. Gulf Coast Brewery offers a diverse selection of brews to wet the palate of any beer drinker. Ales on tap include Changing Tides Cream Ale, English Common Bitter, Sandbar Red Ale, GCB Local Pale Ale, Gulf Coast Light Ale, Sun Love Citrus Ale, Beach Bummed Chocolate Brown Ale, and Sunrise Strawberry Ale. Other options include Karma Driven IPA, Mindbender Double IPA, Laid Back Milk Stout, Pensacola Pilsner Lager, Backstabber Coffee Porter, Coastal Wave Kolsch Style Ale, Hammered Hefeweisen, and Bavarian Dunkelweisen. The only problem Gulf Coast Brewery patrons encounter is deciding which of the myriad premium beers to choose!

But the thing that really sets Gulf Coast Brewery apart is the way it truly involves the community in the brewing process. Unlike some breweries that keep its brewing operation sequestered from the public eye, Gulf Coast Brewery encourages its patrons to take in the experience, learn about the brewing process, and have fun while doing it. The brewing facility is much more than beer production tanks, hot steam generators, and filtration machines—it is a game room, a place for community activities and for entertainment. Located in clear view adjacent to the main entrance, visitors may be intrigued to see a large open room with benches, Ping-Pong tables, and corn hole boards, right next to the brewing operation...where all the magic happens. At the end of the day, one thing is quite evident: Gulf Coast Brewery is the epitome of the marriage of beer production and community entertainment.

Pensacola Bay Brewery

Pensacola Bay Brewery is another unique harbor for folks who fancy drinking their frothy pints in a pleasant, comfortable atmosphere. Founded in 2010, Pensacola Bay Brewery imparts a history lesson with each pour. Located in the heart of historic Downtown Pensacola, the brewpub focuses on Pensacola's rich history, incorporating local landmarks and lore into its beer names and artwork. It is brilliant, really. Pensacola Bay Brewery's proclamation is clear: "We're a city of pirates, conquistadors, fisherman and fighter pilots, who demand beer as strong and complex as we are. Now, we finally have it." Further acknowledging Pensacola's past—with devastating hurricanes, oil spills, and military conquests—the brewery tells patrons and perspective patrons alike, "We make beer that goes down easy, for a city that never has." Indeed, Pensacola pride is perfectly palpable at this prestigious pub.

Pensacola Bay Brewery visitors can expect many things when visiting this charming establishment: good conversation, relaxation, a rich learning experience, and, of course, great beer. Its beer is immensely popular in Pensacola, and it is gaining notoriety across the Southeast. Offering a smorgasbord of tasty taps, the options seem limitless, and the homage to Pensacola's rich and long lasting past is quite evident. For instance, the DeLuna German Style Kolsch, an extra pale ale with a sweet honey-like aroma and a hint of floral hop note, is named for Don Tristan de Luna y Arellano (1519-1573) who established the first settlement in Pensacola in 1559. The Lighthouse Porter, with a dark roast coffee aroma and a taste characterized by roasted malt and chocolate, pays tribute to the Pensacola

Lighthouse, an iconic Pensacola landmark. An array of other Pensacola history inspired names distinguish the rest of Pensacola Bay Breweries additional offerings, from amber ale to imperial stout.

Redneck Riviera Brewing Project

Small? Quite. Relatively unknown? For the time being. Delicious? If it isn't, the next round is on me! For brewers Tim Roberts, Rob Roberts, and Tim Moore, Redneck Riviera Brewing Project—a nano-brewery with macro-devotion—is the manifestation of a long-held, genuine love for supremely crafted beer, the brewing process, and the enjoyment of partaking with friends and family. The Redneck Riviera Brewing Project, which is gaining quite a bit of attention among Pensacola beer enthusiasts, is Pensacola's newest brewpub and brewing education center at the time this book was written. Its primary focus is bringing "top of the line craft beer and brewing education to the Gulf Coast area." Redneck Riviera touts itself as being an organization that is "focused on crafting world-class beers with local flair."

Building upon a friendship that started over a decade ago, Tim Roberts and Larry Cowan—owner/operator of Goat Lips Chew & Brewhouse in Pensacola—joined forces to create something quite special. The dynamic duo converted the old Goat Lips kitchen area to accommodate the brewing operation. This effort was the cornerstone of the Redneck Riviera Brewing Project mission: "Small batch beer...local ingredients...great location...enough said." Short and to the point, their mission is profound far beyond its terseness. Like the other Pensacola-based breweries today, the Goat Lips/Redneck Riviera brewpub is much more than a stool to sit and drink upon. A sanctuary for clientele from all walks of life, Cowan envisioned his deli house as a safe place for University of West Florida students (UWF is close in proximity) to gather and safely enjoy great food and beer. Thus, he ensures that the fun and excitement never ceases. From weekly corn hole pick-up games and team trivia contests to open mic night and live music sessions with house musician Mike Boccia, patrons are never lacking in opportunity to enjoy their pints of Redneck Riviera's finest in an inviting, entertainment-centric environment.

Known for its delicious food and world-class customer service, Goat Lips is equally revered for its awesome beer selection. The clean and comfortable bar room is accommodated with an ample selection of beer in the can or bottle and on tap, but its featured brew derives from the modest yet efficient brewing barrels of Redneck Riviera Brewing Project. Presently, Redneck Riviera—under the auspices of main brewmaster Rob Roberts (Tim's brother and lifelong best friend) offers unique and enjoyable beers in many varieties.

The Sea Oat Pale Ale is smooth and creamy, combining the floral, citrusy flavors of American hops with the mouthfeel of oatmeal. The Argo Amber, the name of which pays homage to the University of West Florida mascot, is not your run of the mill amber. This rich, malty beer is characterized by hints of caramel and toasted nuts with a fresh, crisp, and hoppy finish. Part IPA and part red ale, the #58 Red Ale is in a class of its own. Crafted with the seasoned beer drinker in mind, this bold brew is malty and bitter with hints of floral notes. It will make your tongue slap the roof of your mouth! And last but certainly not least is perhaps the most unique and interesting of all: Sweet Potato Ale. The Redneck Riviera beer family believes that sweet potatoes should not be limited to a Thanksgiving casserole or pie: "We here at RRBP think that sweet potatoes are a vastly underused tuber." So, what did they do? They put them to good use! Through countless trials and drudging experimentation, the folks at Redneck Riviera discovered that adding 42 pounds of sweet potatoes and the right amount of cinnamon, nutmeg, and allspice to a batch of rich, malty amber ale creates the closest thing an adventurous connoisseur can find to a sweet potato pie in a glass. Drink it up!

McGuire's Irish Pub

McGuire's Irish Pub is the oldest of Pensacola's present-day brewing operations. *Feasting. Imbibery. Debauchery.* There could not be three words more suitable for a combination restaurant, pub, and brewery so steeped in history, where the food is befitting a king and the booze flows like water. McGuire's Irish

Pub, which first opened its doors in 1977, offers its patrons much more than the famous *Irish Wake*. First, McGuire's boasts a selection of delicious in-house brews. Among its ales, porters, and stouts—all brewed on premise under the auspices of a renowned brewmaster—patrons can sample any of McGuire's regularly brewed beers, from the McGuire's Light Ale to the

McGUIRE'S IRISH PUB

rich and creamy McGuire's Irish Stout. But these mainstays merely scratch the surface of available beverages.

McGuire's also offers a generous selection of seasonal brews, including, but not limited to, Oktoberfest, Scotch Ale, Honey Wheat, Wild Irish Raspberry Wheat, Belgian Ale, India Pale Ale, Hefeweizen, Extra Special Bitter Altbier, and the immensely popular Christmas Ale. For a period of time, McGuire's also served a potent barley wine, the aptly named *I'll Have What the Gentleman on the Floor is Having*. At 12% alcohol by volume, there is no wonder that gentleman ended up on the floor. Patrons can also join the McGuire's Mug Club to personalize their drinking experience and receive discounted prices on pints. For a small fee, prospective Mug Club members can purchase a one-of-a-kind 16 oz. ceramic stein with unique, personalized inscriptions. On Wednesday nights, Mug Club members can present their fancy steins and drink all night for bargain prices. And members need not worry about remembering to bring their mugs; McGuire's even offers to safely store all Mug Club member steins, free of charge.

For drinkers who prefer beer of the "root variety," McGuire's even brews its own root beer. This delectable G-rated beverage is derived "from the purest natural sassafras root." Adding a scoop of rich vanilla ice cream makes for one epic root beer float! And get this; visitors can even take a tour of the brewery. The brewmaster will be happy to show them around and answer any questions. Homebrewers even have the option to take some of McGuire's yeast to try in their next batch of brew. This is truly a unique opportunity for them to experiment and hone their craft.

So, there is the famous *Irish Wake* and a generous selection of delicious beer always brewed on location. What more could there be? Well, wine, of course! In fact, McGuire's takes its wine very seriously…so seriously that it is home to one of the largest restaurant wine cellars in existence: the world-famous Ruprecht O'Tolf Wine Cellar. Indeed, McGuire's wine cellar has garnered critical acclaim, having received the Wine Spectator's Award of Excellence award on many occasions, including the Wine Spectator's Best of Award of Excellence. Its wine list is all-encompassing, featuring highly rated wines from all over the world, and chosen based on the knowledge of their Certified Sommelier as well as high-profile wine publications, such as Wine Spectator, Wine Enthusiast, and Wine Advocate. Among its 8,000 bottles of fine wine are options with price tags steep enough to present an interesting question: should I buy a bottle of wine or a used car?

Like Pensacola's days of old—the glory days of the alcohol industry, when young German entrepreneurs and American-born moonshiners rose to celebrity status—the alcohol industry of today is still closely linked to social activities. And at McGuire's Irish Pub, the fun, as well as the booze, simply never ends. For example, McGuire's has hosted the Annual St. Patrick's Day Run for nearly 40 years. This charity event has become so immensely popular that, during the start of the race, Gregory Street in Downtown Pensacola transforms from a bustling freeway into a flowing river of green-clad contestants. Every year, thousands of people flock to McGuire's Irish Pub to participate in the 5K run; but this is not your typical 5K. Participants might "carb up" before the green flag waves, but their source of carbs is far more likely to be beer rather than pasta. The St. Patrick's Day Run is predictive rather than fiercely competitive. Participants guess their times, and the closest prediction wins. And face it, when participants are no longer faced with performance pressures and competitive angst, there is a lot more opportunity for some good old fashioned fun. Rather than donning knee-high socks, running shorts, and athletic sneakers, participants are more likely to dress as leprechauns or cartoon characters, or wear green tutus, kilts, or Donegals. Yes, drinking is allowed before, during, and after the race. After all, it is St. Patrick's Day we are talking about here! And after the race, participants make a bee-line for the goodies—*Irish Wakes* and beer to wet the palate and beef and barley stew to satiate the appetite. With its vast selection of brews, its high-quality vintages, and its booze-centric activities, McGuire's continues to carry on Pensacola's long tradition of alcohol-related excellence and entertainment. Let the feasting, imbibery, and debauchery reign supreme!

John D. Melvin, II

ACKNOWLEDGMENTS

This little book is the manifestation of months of archival research, oral histories, and coffee consumption. It began as my master's thesis paper and gradually became something more meaningful and, yes, more aesthetically pleasing. It behooves me to offer my sincere appreciation to some folks for helping move this project from my dreams to the bookshelves. I want to thank Dan Vega, Hamishe Randall, Bobby Dunaway, and the rest of the Indigo River Publishing staff for their helpful and friendly guidance; Danielle I. Upman for her unwavering support and encouragement; and Chris Dunkle, Hunter Brown, Angelia Byers, and Leslie McGill for their editorial assistance.

There were also many people who helped fund this project, so I want to thank the following contributors: Justin Newton, Monty Willis, Dennis Mills, Adrianna Loftus, Tiffany Hanley Flanagan, Justin Oswald, Tim Whiteside, James and Robin Overbay, Trevor Hadder, Elizabeth Dooley, Vickie Melvin (my mom), Misty Melvin (my sister), Mark and EJ Peterson, Jeremy Porter, Allan Buelvas, Pete Silva, Peter Tormey, Billy Schimmel, Rose McKnight (my aunt), Danny McInnes (my cousin), Trent Ciccone, Dr. Josh Branum, Keith Tullius, Burt Douglas, and Jeff Forman.

WORK CITED

Aldridge, Violet. Interview by Elizabeth Vickers. Tape recording. Pensacola, Florida, April 19, 2003. Elizabeth D. Vickers Collection, Special Collections, John C. Pace Library, University of West Florida, Pensacola, Florida.

"Brewery Spreads Pensacola's Praise Throughout District," *The Pensacola News Journal*, October 2, 1949.

Bruington, Lola Lee Daniel. Interview by Sandra F. Whitehead, 1987, Bruington oral history transcripts 1987-10. Special Collections, John C. Pace Library, University of West Florida, Pensacola, Florida.

Chris Thiesen vs. City of Pensacola, 11617-CA-01. Escambia County Archives, Pensacola, Florida.

Counceller, Harry. "Spearman Brewing Company, Part II: The Can Composite," *Beer Can Collector's News Report* 16, no. 6 (November/December 1986).

"The Spearman Brewing Company Part II," *The American Can Collector* 10, no. 79 (November 1986).

"The Spearman Brewing Company," *The American Can Collector* 9, no. 71 (January, 1986).

Deed of Sale from E. E. and Susan A. Simpson to C. Kupfrian, 1870. Deed Book S, pages 246-247. Escambia County Courthouse, Pensacola, Florida.

Deed of Sale from Christian and B. E. Corner to C. Kupfrian, 1878. Deed Book W, page 163. Escambia County Courthouse, Pensacola, Florida.

Deed of Sale from George W. Reab to C. Kupfrian, 1878. Deed Book W, pages 159-161. Escambia County Courthouse, Pensacola, Florida.

Downard, William L. *Dictionary of the History of the American Brewing and Distilling Industries*, (Westport and London: Greenwood Press, 1980).

Halliburton, Arthur. "The Great Oaks Still Stand...but Where," *The Pensacola News*, April 8, 1960.

Jones' Pensacola Directory, 1893-1894 (Pensacola: W. C. & Frank Jones Advertising and Mailing Agency, 1893).

"Liquor Runners May Have Taken Agents in Tow," *The Pensacola Journal*, Thursday, December 2, 1926.

"Local Affairs," *Pensacola Commercial News*, February 25, 1881.

Madden, Joe. *Union Hill Baptist Cemetery*. Accessed October 27, 2008. http://flgenhistonline.com/counties/escambia/cemeteries/union.htm

Maloney's Pensacola City Directory, 1898 (Atlanta: Maloney Directory Company, 1898).

McGovern, James R. *The Emergence of a City in the Modern South: Pensacola 1900-1945* (DeLeon Springs: E. O. Painter Printing Company, 1976).

"Official Programme of First Race Meet Under the Auspices of the West Florida Cycle and Good Roads Club," Friday, October 23, 1896.

Obituary of Capt. Jacob Kryger, *The Pensacola Journal*, October 21, 1908.

Pensacola City Directory, 1896 (Montgomery: Brown Printing Co., Printers and Binders, 1896).

Pfeiffer, Herman. "A Time to Remember," September 1973.

"Home Brew," April 1975.

"Prohibition Daze," February 1975.

"The Days of the Swinging Doors," August 1974.

"The Walls Came Tumbling Down," August 9, 1972.

Public History Resource Center, *Anti-Saloon League 1893-1933*. Accessed October 21, 2008. http://www.publichistory.org/reviews/View_Review.asp?DBID=84

"Prohibition Men Take Big Still," *The Pensacola Journal*, Thursday, November 18, 1926.

R. L. Polk & Co.'s Pensacola Directory, 1905 (Pensacola: R. L. Polk & Co., Publishers, 1905).

R. L. Polk & Co.'s Pensacola Directory, 1907 (Pensacola: R. L. Polk & Co., Publishers, 1907).

"Raiders Continue to Seize Liquor Stills in County," *The Pensacola Journal*, Wednesday, November 17, 1926.

Rosasco III, William S. Letter to Mary Dawkins. February 19, 1996.

St. John's Historic Cemetery, *Pensacola Fishing and Maritime Heritage*. Accessed November 20, 2007. http://www.stjohnshistoriccemetery.com/pensacolas_heritages/fishing.htm

Sutton, Leora M. "Christian Ustrup Thiesen," 1989.

"The Waterfront," 1979.

"The Golden Dream: Life in Pensacola in the 1870's," *Pensacola Historical Society Quarterly* 7, no. 3 (Spring 1974).

"The Spearman Brewery," *Beer Can Collector's News Report* 16, no. 2 (March/April 1986).

Thienel, Phillip. "Kupfrian's Park," *The Escambia County Beacon*, August 26, 1982.

"Kupfrian's Park," *The Escambia County Beacon*, August 5, 1982.

"Kupfrian's Park: At the Turn of the Century," *The Escambia County Beacon*, September 2, 1982.

Watson, J. Brent. "The Barn," date unknown.

Wheeler, Larry. "Barrancas Brewery Bubbled After Prohibition," *The Pensacola News Journal*, March 22, 1984.

Wheeler, Larry. "Park's Memories Disappear with Kupfrian's Life," *The Pensacola News*, May 3, 1984.

Wiggins' Pensacola City Directory, 1903 (Columbus: The Wiggins Directories Publishing Co., 1903).

Wilson, Jacqueline Tracy. *Historic Photos of Pensacola* (Nashville: Turner Publishing Company, 2008).

Pensacola History Bonus: A Note From the Author

I want to personally thank you for purchasing my debut book! When I began my college career at Pensacola Junior College in 2001, I was a prospective mathematics and physics major. I was fascinated by the sciences. Photographs of Werner Heisenberg, Albert Einstein, and the 1927 Solvay Conference adorned the walls in my home office. I took a dual enrollment American history course in high school that changed everything; I quickly developed a new passion. I had recently read a quote attributed to the great Chinese philosopher Confucius (551-479 BC), and it was fresh on my mind when I took that history course: "Choose a job you love, and you will never have to work a day in your life." I assumed I would be taking a significant pay cut, but I did not care. Nothing was going to stop me from studying history in college, and it was one of the best decisions I have ever made!

Many years later, I have found my career in instructional design. I love my profession, and since 2014, I have gained so much knowledge and many valuable skills. I even decided to continue my formal education.

John D. Melvin, II

In 2016, I completed a Graduate Certificate in Online Instructional Development as a student in the Instructional Systems and Learning Technologies program within the College of Education at Florida State University. But, despite my career and continuing education, I consider myself an historian, first and foremost, then an instructional designer. This mentality prompted me to incorporate my background in—and passion for—history into several class projects at Florida State University.

The manifestation of this combination of history and instructional design is a project I would like to share with you. It is a mobile learning enhancement designed to assist historic cemetery visitors to participate in a self-guided walking tour. Impressed with the project, my professor asked me to be a presenter at the 2015 Florida State University Digitech Conference, which is an annual, one-day open-house that offers a venue for students to showcase their computing or digital technology innovations. History aficionados, in general—and Pensacola history lovers, in particular—will enjoy this bit of bonus material.

Historic St. Michael's Cemetery Guided Walking Tour w/ QR Code Implementation

Project Overview:

This project is designed to help facilitate the guided walking tour presented on the information boards at the entrances of St. Michael's Cemetery in Pensacola, Florida. To assist cemetery visitors in taking the guided walking tour, a QR code would be placed at each memorial in the tour. The first QR code, at the information boards near the cemetery entrances, directs the participants to the Guided Tour page of the website, which has a brief introduction to the mobile device-enhanced guided walking tour and a video that virtually walks the visitors to the first site in the tour (the memorial of Stephen R. Mallory). Once the participants arrive at the first destination, they may observe the site and read the historical placard. When they are ready to move on to the next site, they may simply scan the QR code provided at the site, which directs them to the corresponding "Memorials" page of the next memorial in the tour on the website.

Design and Use:

Each memorial page consists of a photograph of the site, a brief historical description, a satellite map with pinpointed location of the site that links to its Google Maps page using precise GPS coordinates, and a video that leads the particpants to the next site in the guided walking tour. Since there is a "back-end support" component in a stand-alone website, the mobile learning concept is flexible. Participants are presented with essentially three ways to participate in this learning experience: 1.) They may either start at the information boards and work their way through the guided walking tour by scanning all the QR codes, 2.) they may simply work their way through the guided walking tour by physically navigating through the website on their mobile devices, or 3.) they may utilize the QR codes/website on an "as needed" basis as they take their own tour, including sites that may not be included in the list of "Points of Interest."

Technologies Used:

I purchased the domain name www.historicstmichaelscemetery.com and created the website using WordPress. The tour guidance video clips were created using Instagram's Hyperlapse app, and provided through Vimeo's video sharing infrastructure. Hyperlapse allowed me to created short, stabilized and hyperlapsed video clips, implemented to guide tour participants from site to site, eliminating any guess work and confusion involved in looking at a static map. Vimeo proved to be a preferred alternative to YouTube in this project.

Vimeo videos are easily imbedded into WordPress websites, and tools are provided for including video titles and selecting frames for thumbnail image use. I also utilized Acceleroto's GPS Location app to provide precise GPS coordinates for each location.

Future Plans:
I initially created this mobile learning enhancement by creating a website for information presentation. For now, the delivery is perfectly adequate, and the website is easily navigated, easy to understand, and simple to use. The next step involves converting the website into a mobile app.

Unique Features:
This project's most unique feature is the incorporation of Vimeo provided videos—produced using Instagram's Hyperlapse app, for image stabilization and hyperlapsing—which lead guided tour participants from site to site throughout the tour. Additionally, I utilized Acceleroto's GPS Location app to provide precise GPS coordinates for each location. Participants may access the sites' Google Maps pages, and view the pinpointed location of any site in the tour in satellite view. This mobile learning enhancement is extremely valuable, as it provides cemetery visitors with all the tools necessary for adequately participating in the existing self-guided walking tour. St. Michael's Cemetery covers approximately eight acres, with some 3200 marked grave sites, and without the guidance afforded by this learning enhancement, participants are

presented with a daunting task. Indeed, the tour's value is lost when participants struggle to locate the "Points of Interest."

Website Components:

The website can be easily navigated by selecting one of the main menu options at the top of the screen. The following descriptions and screenshots show each section of the website.

Welcome

This is the landing spot upon arrival at the main website.

Memorials

Located in the heart of historic Downtown Pensacola, Florida, St. Michael's Cemetery covers approximately eight acres of land and contains over 3,000 marked grave sites. The cemetery, which dates to the late 18th century, showcases Pensacola's rich and diverse history. St. Michael's Cemetery tells a fascinating story about the history of America's oldest settlement. To learn more about the history of this historic site, visit the St. Michael's Cemetery official website.

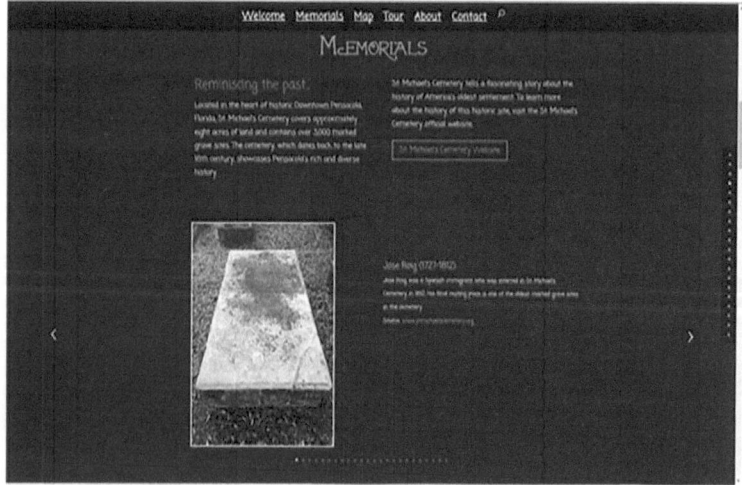

Interactive Map

This interactive map provides a satellite view of St. Michael's Cemetery with markers showing the precise location of each point of interest in the guided walking tour.

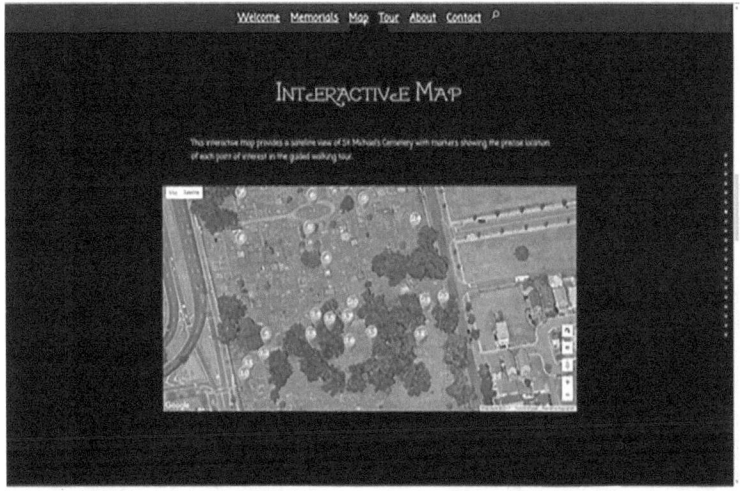

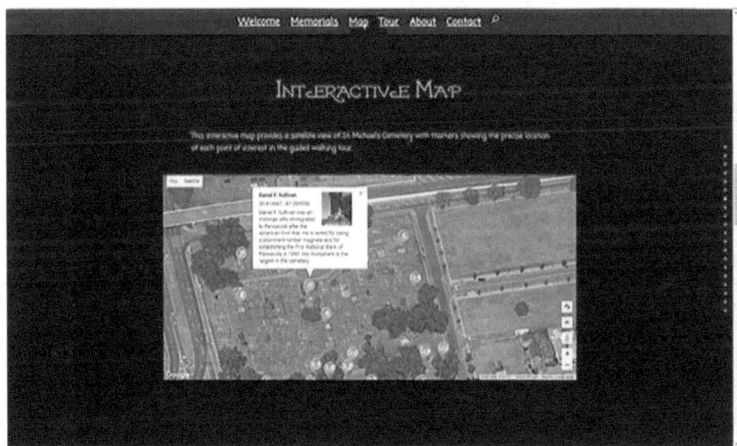

Interactive Map Page (with site marker selected)

Guided Walking Tour

To assist you in taking the guided walking tour, you can begin at the Guided Walking Tour section below, which has a brief introduction to the mobile device-enhanced guided walking tour and a video that virtually walks you to the first site in the tour (the memorial of Stephen R. Mallory). Once you arrive at the first destination, you may observe the site and read the historical placard. When you are ready to move on to the next site, simply select the nice site, which directs you to the corresponding "Memorials" page of the next memorial.

Click on the video below to begin the tour! You will be guided to the first memorial in the tour: Stephen R. Mallory.

John D. Melvin, II

About St. Michael's

St. Michael's Cemetery is an eight-acre green space in the heart of urban, historic Pensacola, Florida. Probably in use by the mid to late 18th century, the land was officially designated a cemetery by the King of Spain in 1807. Although initially assigned to the CatholAic inhabitants of Pensacola, people of all faiths have traditionally been buried here. The cemetery is an open-air museum that is a testament to the diverse history of Pensacola.

Today, the cemetery is managed by the St. Michael's Cemetery Foundation of Pensacola, Inc., whose mission is to provide overall management, support restoration and conservation efforts that maintain the historic fabric of the site, and promote public awareness and stewardship through education. The nonprofit foundation works with the University of West Florida and many community groups and individuals to preserve this historic site.

Source: www.stmichaelscemetery.org

Pouring A Round Of Pensacola's Past

If you are in the Pensacola area and love local history, you should make it a point to visit historic St. Michael's Cemetery. Take the walking tour. Use my website. Have fun!

www.ingramcontent.com/pod-product-compliance
Lightning Source LLC
Chambersburg PA
CBHW020621300426
44113CB00007B/734